YOUR KNOWLEDGE HAS VALUE

Charae Tongg

Masochism in Franz Kafka's "Metamorphosis"

GRIN Verlag

Bibliografische Information der Deutschen Nationalbibliothek:

Die Deutsche Bibliothek verzeichnet diese Publikation in der Deutschen National-bibliografie; detaillierte bibliografische Daten sind im Internet über http://dnb.d-nb.de/ abrufbar.

Imprint:

Copyright © 2014 GRIN Verlag GmbH
Druck und Bindung: Books on Demand GmbH, Norderstedt Germany
ISBN: 978-3-656-66608-0

GRIN - Your knowledge has value

Der GRIN Verlag publiziert seit 1998 wissenschaftliche Arbeiten von Studenten, Hochschullehrern und anderen Akademikern als eBook und gedrucktes Buch. Die Verlagswebsite www.grin.com ist die ideale Plattform zur Veröffentlichung von Hausarbeiten, Abschlussarbeiten, wissenschaftlichen Aufsätzen, Dissertationen und Fachbüchern.

Visit us on the internet:

http://www.grin.com/

http://www.facebook.com/grincom

http://www.twitter.com/grin_com

Masochism in *The Metamorphosis*

Franz Kafka's *The Metamorphosis* presents the story of Gergor Samsa's disturbing transformation into a bug, which strains both the relationships between other characters in the story with Gregor and the relationship Gregor has with himself. Through the characters' actions in light of Gregor Samsa's change, Franz Kafka not only reveals the dynamic symbiosis between a person's need to feel both pleasure and pain, but seems to also use this knowledge in the very construction of this narrative to manipulate his readers. With the narrative written from Gregor's perspective, presenting Gregor's internal narrative and though, the true extent of submission to others that Gregor practices is understood, like how he submits to the suffering at a miserable job, or when we surrenders as a victim to his buggy condition rather than attempting to better his situation.

Gregor Samsa is revealed as a masochist from the very beginning of the story. From the first few paragraphs of *The Metamorphosis* Kafka portrays that Gregor is shy, lacks self confidence, and rather than - having just awoken as a giant bug - address his transformation as many another protagonist might, he immediately explores feelings of self-hate, isolation and inadequacy. It is almost as the transformation does not put Gregor in a place far from his norm, as he finds the actuality of it far more acceptable than do his peers. Furthermore, before Gregor has even managed to get out of bed, we learn that his drive is not to find pleasure for himself, but rather for others, in such a way that Gregor is only convinced is sufficient if it involves pain and suffering on his part. For example, when describing what his employment is like he describes it as an "exhausting job," (2) where he has no friends, sense of security or regularity and where his employer "[sits] on high at a desk and [talks] down to employees" (2). However, rather than attempt to resolve these issues or find new employment he continues both working there and dwelling in his dislike for it. It would even seem that this abusive environment motivates Gregor and that his fear of failing there drives him every day to same misery. Gregor states that his main motivation for his employment situation is for his family - to pay off their debts - but we see then that his family does not act gratefully, but rather they expect this of him. So even if his motivation is to help his family, it is one more similar to an obligation or servancy. This passive, accepting behavior can be described as indicative of a masochist[1]. Gregor continues to hypnotically work at a miserable job that not he, but his father selected for him, cowering under his employers, for the sake of his ungrateful family. Considering that Gregor could either choose to not help his family or at least do so in a different employment, it seems as though this character does truly want to or feel the need to suffer.

The next example of Gregors helpless devotion to suffering for the sake of others is his withdrawal from the world after his bug-itude. We know that Gregors actions before the transformation were self-suffering and driven to appease others, but this behavior continues afterwards too, when he reveals the shame of being so nonhuman - the shame that would bring to his family and to his employment. So, in response, he lives in solitude to save the public from the distress of interaction with a bug-monster. He proceeds to never leave his bedroom, and even spares his little sister when she comes into feed him as he "not without a slight feeling of shame, he [had] scutted under the sofa." (13) In this act of reclusion, Gregor demonstrates a basic instinct to suffer in shaming himself in order to prevent the suffering of others.

The most important and certainly defining event in Gregor's martyrdom is his demonstration of the most masochistic act humanly possible; death. In the last, pathetic moments of Samsa's condition he performs the ultimate sacrifice for love and by his death, the Gregor family is finally able to thrive. "Then all three left [of the Samsas] the apartment together, which was more than they had done for months"

---

[1] Masochism is often used to describe a sexual tendency, but here and throughout this essay it refers only to the desire to suffer to find gratification.

(33) and upon finding a new house for the family there was "the greatest immediate improvement in their condition." (33) Here the tone switches for the first time in the story form a dreary hopelessness to something hopeful and resolved. Kafka uses vocabulary new to the story like "warm sunshine" (33) and "not bad at all"(33). It is evident by the dramatic change in descriptive style that only at this point in the story - where Samsa experiences the most expensive suffering does he finally admit that his family has benefitted from his actions - that he had finally done enough as a self proclaimed martyr. Kafka found it necessary even to include in this positive toned ending a jab at Samsa after death when he notes that the Samsa's new apartment was "better situated and more easily run than the one they had, which Gregor has selected," specifying that the previous was less suitable and a result of Gregor's presence. This ending is - like the rest of the narrative - told in Gregor's perspective, so whether or not the family was actually miserable before his death (either before or after the metamorphosis) or if that was just a skewed reflection of Gregor's feelings of inadequacy, we know at least that Gregor truly did believe that the greater he suffered, the better off others were - so paired with his death he presented the Samsa family at their peak.

It is evident that Gregor (and Kafka) believed that an exterior happiness was produced through an internal suffering, it should be noted that though Gregor was a suffering character, it was this suffering that satisfied him. In other words, in order to feel pleasure Gregor needed to feel pain. It seems that Kafka is presenting the idea that the two - pain and pleasure - are interdependent. This prevalent theme of the necessity of pain for there to be pleasure throughout the Metamorphosis indicates a bigger idea about the human species. Humans generally tend to categorize any type of suffering as bad and avoidable - we push them away, exorcise them, but really they are natural - even vital - to the human experience. A person must hunger before he can placate, thirst before he can quench, exhaust before he can sleep. These are seemingly basic ideas, but the pairs are absolute, because without the painful feeling you will not have the pleasurable. In addition to presenting the existence of this relationship, *The Metamorphosis* provides further evidence that specifically, the extent of suffering yields proportional satisfaction, again in reference to Gregor's death paired with the Samsa family's success.

It seems as though Kafka did not create this pain-seeking character unintentionally, for after accepting the duality of pain and pleasure presented by the character Gregor Samsa, it appears that Kafka understands this dynamic as one that is present in all humans and uses the text itself to play on this desire to suffer. Kafka starts the story like many others, presenting an issue - Gregor's metamorphosis into a bug - but as the text progresses rather than attempt to resolve this issue, he dances around it - explores it - breeding the reader's anxiety with each new word. The further one reads into the text, the more uncomfortable and anxious they become, which drives them harder to, not close the book, but keep reading with the hope that there will be resolve or relief for the story. Kafka knows we will keep reading and in the end this story does little to satisfy the discontent it causes. Strangely enough, it is this denial of satisfaction in that draws attention to our enslavement to the same masochistic tendencies with which Gregor suffers.

Works Cited

Kaftka, Franz. *Metaphorphosis*. New Haven: Yale University Press, 1996.